JAMES CHARLES: BORN TO BREAK BOUNDARIES

JAMES CHARLES: BORN TO BREAK BOUNDARIES

Aunt Lollie Connie

ISBN: 1978483856
ISBN 13: 9781978483859

J ames Charles was never a typical kid. This was evident early
on. Christie and Ken, James' parents, allowed me to help
write down some early stories specific to James, complete with
matching photographs. As James' aunt, I was lucky to have wit-
nessed some of the events first hand. Although James was too
young to remember most of the details, he gave his permission to
share the content.

Christie was quite discouraged that baby James was not sleep-
ing through the night. At first I thought, she is a new mom, this
is what happens … babies don't sleep, and parents don't sleep.

But she knew it was more than that. I would joke that he didn't sleep, because he had too much on his mind and was already trying to figure out the world. James often had a serious look on his face, as though he was deep in thought. Christie talked to the pediatrician, she read books, she tried evidence-based practices like the Ferber method. The standard techniques did not help. James' pediatrician, Dr. Schumacher, explained that James has a "strong personality," and no one is going to tell him what to do. She warned that he would not be an easy child to parent, but "someday he will do great things." I remember Dr. Schumacher's words, not because I was there, but because Christie shared the doctor's assessment. I remember thinking, the doctor is right. I remind Christie many times- including last week- "Try not to worry about James, it will be okay. Remember what Dr. Schumacher said. Remember what Dr. Schumacher said." When I ask her to look back on this now, she laughs a bit but still looks horrified as she remembers that it wasn't until he was two and a half that he first slept through the night. Whenever she was around new parents, she would ask, "How long before YOUR baby slept through the night?" There were various answers, but she never found anyone to commiserate with. No one was close to two and a half years!

James could clearly say "Dr. Schumacher" at 18 months, and he was saying 15 word sentences at age two. He was precocious and articulate. At age two, he knew that the green leggy bug on the front of his picture book was not a mere grasshopper, as someone erroneously told him. "No," he corrected, "that is a praying mantis."

James is strong willed and more intense than most. His persistence was evident early on. Christie doesn't remember the details of the disagreement, but she explained that when James was two years old, she said "No" to something, as all good parents must. James did not stop arguing. She argued with him a bit and then realized, "I must stop or it won't end" ... so she tried to ignore him. She walked into another room, sat down, took a deep breath, and put the newspaper up to her face, hoping he would find something else to do. But James could not or would not let it go. *Flick, flick, flick* at the newspaper with his toddler finger. *Flick, flick, flick* ... Almost as if saying, "I would like to continue this debate."

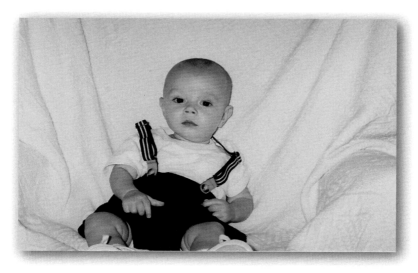

During another disagreement, James was sent to the "time out" chair. Christie's reference book recommended one minute for each year of age. James should have been in time out for two minutes, but he refused to give up the fight. The rule was, if you talk back, a minute is added. Fifteen minutes later, he was still in time out and still arguing his case. Due to his persistent and sassy comments, he was in time out that day for 17 straight minutes.

Christie has used words such as persistent, determined, and spirited to describe James. The word that comes to my mind is *intractable*. I heard the word on a vocabulary strengthening tape in 2004 and remembered the definition by associating it with James ... not necessarily in a bad way, but let's face it, he wanted to manage himself even as a young child.

3

At two and a half years old, James stayed with his grandparents while Christie was busy bringing his baby brother, Ian, into the world. Sitting on the couch peering out into the driveway, with a very serious look on his face, he asked his grandmother, "Mimi, how old must you be to drive?" He had never been away from his mother and had his sights set on driving to see her. Mimi still talks about this, remembering how funny it was to hear a toddler ask such an adult thing. Where did he come up with that? It was evident early on that James has an internal locus of control. He believes that events are caused by controllable factors such as one's attitude, preparation, and effort (not to mention persistence!) In other words, if you want something to happen, you don't just wait and see if it happens, you make it happen.

Aunt Lollie Connie

4

James has always been creative, driven, and focused in his pursuits. When he finds something he is passionate about, he is determined to be successful. James' favorite conventional toys were K'nex and Legos. He would sit for hours on end, putting together the tiny pieces until the project was complete. James did not spend too much time looking at toys in the toy store or department store. His interest was vacuum cleaners, power cords, and other electrical items. I bought many of his birthday presents at Home Depot ... one year I was happy to indulge him with his very own UL-listed, standard yellow, contractor-grade extension cord. Because Ken was concerned that James would not be able to resist trying out the actual electrical outlets, he built James his very own safe "electrical box." The outlets were not actually connected to anything live but still fun to play with. This also helped keep the cords in one place rather than wrapped around the staircase balusters. (There is a photo of one of James' early creative designs, electrical cords tied around frying pans.) I remember thinking, maybe he will be an electrician or inventor. Who knew that just a few years later, his lighting interest would be all about selfies, videos, and glam shots.

James' interest in vacuum cleaners was not short-lived. Most preschoolers, who enjoyed the Teletubbies television series, could purchase their favorite tubby in the form of a plush toy, backpack, or hard plastic keyring, because they were focused on one or all four main characters of differing colors. James, however, was focused on the blue vacuum cleaner, Noo noo, a supporting character in the same show. While the four Teletubbies puttered around their earth house and garden making delightful communicative noises, Noo noo, who had a sucker like nose, made slurping noises as he cleaned the house. Although Noo noo didn't have as much screen time, he was the most exciting to James.

James was almost four years old when he visited an aquarium with his family. He asked numerous questions while he enjoyed watching the sea creatures swim behind the glass enclosures. He moved through each exhibit with ease, until the diver emerged holding the underwater vacuum cleaner. This was cause for an extra level of excitement, with a steadier stream of questions, making it more difficult to lure James away. His intense interest was photo-worthy.

Even haircuts were about vacuum cleaners. While most kids were bribed with candy for sitting still, James was focused on the numerous vacuum cleaners and accessories in the hairdresser's closet. "If you sit still for Tracy, she will help you pull out all the vacuum cleaners in her closet." A deal was made. She had a large canister vacuum, a lighter stick model, and handheld vacuums that came with their own wall mount. For a mere ten minutes of sitting still, James earned five minutes of vacuum cleaner inspection. Most even came with electrical cords.

When James was three years old, he still used a bebe at night time. By bebe, I mean rubber pacifier. I guess bebe means blanket to some people, but James' bebe was his pacifier. Christie wanted him to relinquish his bebe, so she fibbed. She made up a story, not unlike the tooth fairy idea. It went something like this...

Christie: "Tonight we are not going to take the bebe to bed. We are going to put the bebe in a box and leave it on the front porch for the Bebe Fairy. She will take it and leave you a present."

James: "Why does she need to take it?"

Christie: "Because there are new babies being born all the time, and they need that bebe."

James' valid comeback: "But my bebe would be too big for them."

Christie's great ad-lib: "Well yes, that is true, but the Bebe Fairy has a bebe shrinking machine. She will shrink your bebe so it is small enough for the new born babies."

I guess that was a good enough answer, because he agreed to give up the bebe in exchange for a gift. His requested prize was a Shark vacuum cleaner. Christie remembers being terrified that first night. She was thinking, I have a kid that has a history of sleep difficulties, and I am taking away the thing that helps him sleep every night. Is this worth it? James slept fine, probably dreaming of his Shark.

I visited James soon after the Bebe Fairy delivered his Shark. He couldn't wait to share in the delight of his new device. "Do you want to suck up crumbs with me Aunt Lollie Connie? C'mon, do you want to?"

5

There is a photograph of four-year-old James, in his soccer uniform, warming up for the game with sideline cartwheels. Christie remembers him running away from the playing field soon after the game started. Maybe he knew soccer wasn't his thing, and maybe he realized he could still make the best of this from the sidelines. He took it upon himself to be the assistant coach. When the coach yelled out an order, he parroted the coach's instructions with emphasis. James enjoyed taking the lead and keeping things organized. Christie told me a similar story about him from pre-school. The teacher instructed the students to come to the red rug area for story time. James noticed that not everyone was following the rule. He chimed in, like a little sheep herder, "Come on kids, come over to the red rug."

04-29-05

James signed up for the Kindergarten t-ball team. There is a nice picture of him smiling, as he readied his swing. As any good teammate knows, while on the bench, you cheer on your team and wait your turn. James also found time to socialize with his bench mates. One bench mate, Gabby, had beautiful long hair. Christie tells a story about the day she noticed James on the bench, uninterested in the game, chatting intently with Gabby, as he braided her hair. T-ball, like soccer, was not going to be a favorite activity.

6

I asked my sister to re-tell me the story about James and his public speaking debut. He was four. It happened the first day, in the first ten minutes at summer day camp. James was the youngest kid there. About 40 people, including parents, gathered around for the opening of the week-long day camp. The organizer asked for a volunteer to come up front and share what they did over the weekend. Christie didn't think James would want to talk in front of so many new faces, but he was delighted to take the microphone. It was an electronic device with a cord, after all. He started with the commentary like a little pro, going on and on about his recent trip to Cape Cod. He smiled, looked around at all the faces, and told his story with confidence.

7

James Charles always knew just what he wanted, and nine times out of ten, he figured out a way to get it. In 2006, I asked my nieces and nephews to participate in creating a time capsule. I interviewed each child separately and recorded their answers to a series of questions. I tucked the responses in an envelope, wrote DO NOT OPEN UNTIL 2016, and hid the envelope in my parents' closet for safekeeping. During the 2016 holidays, we all had a good laugh as we read through each child's responses. James predicted he would be living in California and studying science and discovery. I am not sure if makeup is considered a science, but James is certainly busy discovering his potential. Even at the age of seven, James had his sights set on a bright future living in California.

8

J ames' artistic talent was a common theme throughout his childhood. In his second-grade art class, James used ink and pastels to draw a fall-themed still life with pumpkins and gourds. His creation was chosen by his teacher to be on display at the local art show.

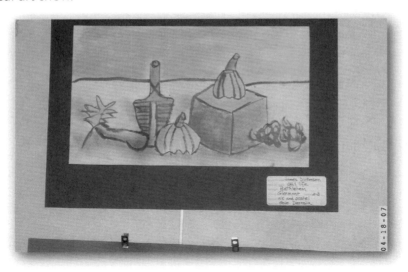

In fourth grade, James designed a doll prototype and asked his mother to help sew several samples to sell at school. Christie gently broke the news to him saying something like, this probably won't work, I don't think you are supposed to sell things at school. Christie was wrong. James came home from school that very day with several orders, including one from a teacher.

While in fifth grade, James' t-shirt design won first place and ended up being his classmates' graduation attire on their last day of elementary school. He drew a globe above a pair of hands with the words, "It's in our hands."

When he reached ninth grade, James' advanced math skills earned him a 100% on the tenth-grade geometry statewide Regents' exam. The reward for a perfect grade was an opportunity to have the teacher wear a t-shirt of the student's choosing. James designed a shirt endorsing his YouTube subscription information and marketing his weekly videos. Sound familiar?

9

In the spring of 2016, when James was a junior in high school, Christie was asked by the school Guidance Counselor to write down her thoughts about James' leadership skills in preparation for college. She wrote, "James is a natural born leader. He is a passionate, tenacious individual who does not take 'no' for an answer. He has been an entrepreneur since I can remember. Several years ago, he made a profit by selling his Instagram account because of the number of followers he had. Last year he was successful by building up a clientele to style hair for special events. In November of 2015, James started his makeup artistry and is now known all over the internet for his creative style."

Probably because she tried to outsmart James many times throughout the years, Christie didn't remember this last story until I reminded her. You know those claw crane arcade games – known as merchandisers – commonly found in malls and the alleyways of grocery stores? These *vending machines* consist of prizes, usually plush toys or alternatives such as capsuled toys or candy. You insert your money and turn the crank to operate the claw like metal contraption. The claw moves around, usually only once, and may or may not stop over a prize. The worst part is, even if the claw lands directly over a prize, it never seems to have enough grip strength to grasp and carry the darn thing to the out door. We found one, full of candy, near the bathroom as we waited for Ken to finish his hockey game in a local arena. This machine was different because it touted, "Play until you win." Wow, this is great, we thought. Ten minutes later, Christie and I were still taking turns trying to get the claw to work as toddler James Charles, watching intently from his stroller, waited for one of the candy pieces to come out of the hatch. We wanted to give up, but James wouldn't let us. In a flash of brilliance, Christie realized she had a lollipop in her purse that looked exactly like one of the possible prizes. I distracted James, while she stuffed her hand and the lollipop into the dispenser. Then she yipped with joy, so James would turn his head back at the exact moment her hand was seemingly coming out with a new prize. We won! I think I remember the incident, because I was so impressed by Christie's on-the-spot ingenuity.

Some people may say, why didn't you let him get disappointed, he needs to learn. That is certainly a valid point. Christie and Ken said "No" many times, but they also learned to pick and choose their battles. There is a quote by Sarah Stogryn, affixed to the family room bulletin board in their home. "Strong-willed children become adults who change the world, as long as we can hang on for the ride and resist the temptation to 'tame' the spirit out of them." Believing in Dr. Schumacher's early assessment, lots of deep breathing, and embracing the Stogryn quote helped pave the way for James to become the person he is today. James Charles is certainly making a difference with his passion, courage, and creativity.

Buckle your seat-belt and enjoy the ride, because James' journey has only just begun...

Made in the USA
Middletown, DE
05 December 2018